THE STORY OF WITCHES

OTHER BOOKS BY THE AUTHOR

THE STORY OF Witches

THOMAS G. AYLESWORTH

Illustrated with old prints

McGRAW-HILL BOOK COMPANY

New York · St. Louis · San Francisco · Montreal · Toronto

For all the people in Rochester, Indiana

123456789 RABP 7832109

Library of Congress Cataloging in Publication Data

Aylesworth, Thomas G
  The story of witches.
  Bibliography: p.
  Includes index.
  SUMMARY: Discusses how to become a witch, tests used to discover
witches, tools of trade, famous trials, and people who wanted to be
witches.
  1. Witchcraft—Juvenile literature. [1. Witchcraft] I. Title.
BF1566.A92   133.4   79-12321
ISBN 0-07-002649-1

TABLE OF CONTENTS

The Abomination of the Sorcerers. A sixteenth-century print by Jasper Isaac showing a busy little group of witches.

1
A SHORT HISTORY

What do you think of when you think of a witch? Is it an old, ugly woman riding on a broomstick? Does she hang around with a cat all the time?

That's the usual Halloween costume witch. But there are a few things wrong with the idea. In the first place, many men were said to be witches in the old days. And even children as young as eight years old were put on trial for witchcraft.

Also, not everyone thought that witches could fly through the air. And a cat was only one of several kinds of pets that witches could have.

Or do you think of a witch as being like the old hag in *Hansel and Gretel*? That's not too accurate, either. Actually, she wasn't cruel enough. Didn't she feed Hansel well? And what's so wrong with pinching him every now and then to see if he was putting on a few pounds? (Even if she did want to eat him.)

No, the people of long ago had a much different idea of what a witch was supposed to be. First of all, the witch was a servant of the Devil. That meant that he or she was truly evil. Also, witches didn't need to wear funny clothes. Your next-door neighbor could be one, and you might not know it.

Today, of course, hardly anybody believes in evil witchcraft. We think we are very modern. But it might surprise you to find out that, up until the 1200's, most people did not think that there were evil witches. This was true even though the Bible says in the book of

Exodus, "Thou shalt not permit a witch to live."

Oh, they believed in magicians and sorcerers. And if they thought about witches at all, they put them in the same group as magicians. They could probably cast spells. Or ruin crops. Or start thunderstorms. Or brew up love potions. But most people did not believe that they could fly through the air or do business with the Devil. Whatever they did, they were doing for their own gain, not the Devil's.

Even though they were not thought to be too harmful, they might be nuisances. So eventually laws were passed against witchcraft and sorcery. Theodosius, one of the last rulers of the Roman Empire, passed one in 381. He called it a crime to conduct witch meetings and perform sacrifices in the old Roman temples.

Theodore, the Archbishop of Canterbury in 690, also worried about witches. He ordered the people to stop casting spells and worshipping demons.

Even then, punishments for practicing witch-craft could be serious. In 580, Fredegund, queen of a part of what is now Germany, lost two of her sons. They really died of a disease called dysentery, but the queen didn't believe that.

She blamed one of her stepsons—Clovis. Fredegund said that he had asked his mother-in-law to cast a spell on the boys. The woman was tortured until she confessed, and then burned to death. Clovis got off a little easier. He was just stabbed to death.

By the time that the 700's came along, people started thinking about what witches did not have the power to do. St. Boniface said that witches could not change into wolves. In the 800's, St. Agobard, the Bishop of Lyons in France, went further. He said that witches could not control the weather or destroy crops. He also said that they could not give people the evil eye. (The evil eye was supposed to be a way of causing harm just by looking at the victim.)

Burning was a popular way to execute witches. This is an engraving made in 1583.

At the same time, the Church in Ireland laid down a rule. Churchgoers received heavy penance if they confessed to a belief in witchcraft. This was especially true if the confession included a belief in broomstick riding and vampirism.

If witches could change themselves into animals, why couldn't they fly, too? A fifteenth-century print by Ulrich Molitor.

In the 900's, a Canon Law of the Church was introduced. It talked about the belief that there were witches who rode beasts in the night and were able to go great distances before dawn.

The law went on to say that anyone who believed that witches could go night flying was "beyond doubt an infidel and a pagan." A little over four hundred years later, anyone who did *not* believe in witches and night flying could be burned at the stake by the Church.

The witch panic began in the early 1400's. People all over Europe seemed to see a wicked witch around every corner. Those poor innocent people who were accused of witchcraft were burned by the hundreds of thousands. Even so, people still kept imagining that more and more of them were wandering the streets or flying through the air.

That was during the time that we often call the Middle Ages. It was a time of horrible epidemics of disease and hunger. There were political and religious disorders. And the

Church began to think that anyone who disagreed with its teachings must be a witch.

The point was that if you didn't believe in the established religion, you must believe in the teachings of the Devil. Soon witches were thought of as serving the Devil. They were enemies of the Church.

Toward the end of the 1400's judges were appointed by the Church and by their governments to try witches. Court records show that there seemed to be more witches in Europe and Scotland than there were in England. At least, more of them confessed there than in England.

The reason for this is that torture was never very popular in England. Only the highest courts could order an accused witch to be tortured. That meant that Scottish and European witches confessed under torture just so that they would be killed quickly. English witches were executed, too. But often they were not tortured, so they died without confessing. They were, however, just as "guilty" as if they had confessed.

Your first idea about this is probably that the judges were terrible, cruel men. But they thought that they were doing the work of the Church in fighting the Devil. One of these priestly judges, Nicolas Remy, had nearly nine hundred French people burned at the stake in the fifteen years from 1575 to 1590. He didn't feel any guilt about it until near the end of his life.

Now don't think that he worried about the people he had caused to be executed. He was worrying about the children that he did not execute. He said that it was not right to "spare baby vipers." They would grow up to be adult witches.

Pierre Binsfield, the Bishop of Treres, France may have been the champion of witch hunters. He sentenced some six thousand, five hundred people to death by burning.

Even Queen Elizabeth I of England was a sort

of witch hunter. In 1563, she issued a law that read: "If any person or persons after the said first day of June, shall use, practise, or exercise witchcraft, enchantment, or sorcery, whereby any person shall happen to be killed or destroyed, they shall suffer pains of death as a Felon or Felons."

By the end of the 1600's, it is estimated that two hundred thousand people had been executed for witchcraft in Europe. One hundred thousand of these executions happened in Germany alone. For example, the Bishop of Würtzburg burned more than nine hundred people in only eight years.

France and Scotland accounted for ten thousand deaths. It seems that only Sweden was relatively free of the witchcraft madness.

Certainly America was not immune. Witches were hanged here, rather than burned. But many of them were executed. The first execution in America was that of Alse Young. This happened in Hartford, Connecticut on May 26,

1647. Three others were hanged in Connecticut and one in Maryland. In Massachusetts, there were hangings in Charlestown, Boston, and Dorchester. Salem, however, is the town you think of when you think of American witchcraft. But more of that later.

Finally, the three-hundred-year nightmare was over. By the end of the 1600's the fear of witches was pretty much a thing of the past. Here is the scorecard showing the year when the last witch was executed in various countries:

The Netherlands	1610
England	1684
America	1692
Scotland	1727
France	1745
Germany	1775

But the English seemed to play it safe. Britain's Witchcraft Act was not repealed until 1951.

2
THE INITIATION

For some reason or other, at least since the 1400's, there have always been large groups of people who wanted to be witches. And that means that for several centuries, there have been ways of being initiated into witches' organizations. Some of the techniques were simple. Some were complicated. But there were usually two requirements.

The first requirement was that the future witch must join of his or her own free will. The second was that he or she must be willing to worship the Devil.

You have to realize one thing. These ancient witches were different from modern-day witches. They looked upon the Devil as their god. Modern witches usually believe in God. They do not worship the Devil.

So the witches of old knelt to the Devil, prayed to the Devil, and offered thanks to him. Sometimes they even dedicated their children to the Devil.

Some witches claimed that the Devil had visited them. But they never could agree on

Here is the Devil taking a child away from his parents. It was all part of a promise that they had made to him. A fifteenth-century German print.

The Devil could take on many forms. Here he is preaching to some witches in Scotland. A sixteenth-century Scottish print.

what he looked like. Sometimes he was supposed to have feet like a goat. Sometimes he looked like a man or a woman. Sometimes he wore strange costumes. Sometimes he walked and sometimes he rode a horse.

His costumes would vary. There were tales of the Devil being dressed in rags or in a fine suit. He occasionally wore black, and at other times he wore a coat of many colors.

He could be old or young. He could be handsome or ugly. He could call himself by any name he chose. Some of these names, in addition to the Devil, were Satan, Lucifer, the Foul Fiend, Beelzebub, the Prince of Evil, or the Enemy of Salvation. He could also choose simpler names. One witch reported that the Devil called himself Daniel, and another witch claimed that he had taken the name Thom Reid.

There were times when he was in the form of a monster, wearing a black gown and a black hat. He was described as having cloven hooves, a nose shaped like an eagle's beak, and huge, burning eyes. His legs were hairy, his hands were like claws.

The Devil also might take the form of an animal. In most places, his favorite disguise was that of a bull, a cat, a dog, or a horse. But in France he seemed to prefer looking like a goat or a sheep.

For some reason he never took the form of a rabbit. This is unusual, since the rabbit was a favorite animal of witches. They were said to be able to change themselves into rabbits whenever they wanted. Also, the Devil did not take the form of a toad. Yet the toad was a common animal used by witches when they performed magic. Finally, the Devil seemed not to like appearing as a fox, a donkey, or a pig.

No one could really believe these transformations today. But when the witches were operating a few hundred years ago, people were much more superstitious. And no witch would ever admit that the Devil—his or her lord and master—could not change his shape.

Anyway, the Devil was essential to the initiation of a witch. Even if he was really a human dressed in a strange costume.

The ceremony of initiation was sometimes a very simple one. In 1594 there was a young French girl who claimed that she had taken a shortcut. Her boyfriend, it turned out, was a witch. And he introduced her to the Devil. All

The Devil also was supposed to have strange powers. This seventeenth-century print shows some of the things that he was supposed to be able to do.

Saducismus Triumphatus.
Part the Second

Fairthorne fec

she had to do to become a witch was to make the sign of the cross with her left hand.

Another method was a bit more complicated. First, the witch-to-be takes a knife that has never been used. Then the knife is used to cut a branch off a wild nut tree that has never borne fruit. This cut must be made at the moment when the morning sun appears on the horizon.

Next, find a bloodstone. This is a type of rock that is basically green, with red spots on it. Take the stone, the branch, and two consecrated candles to a spot where you will not be disturbed. Draw a triangle on the ground with the stone. Put the candles in the dirt next to the triangle and light them.

Now you must stand in the middle of the triangle and wave the branch. And all the time you pray to the Devil. It was said that he would visit you and turn you into a witch.

Most of the time, though, the initiation was supposed to be a much more complicated ceremony.

The initiation of a witch. He denies Christ; is rebaptized; gives the Devil some of his own clothes; and swears allegiance. His name is put into the Book of Death. He agrees to sacrifice children, and gets a "Devil's Mark."

19

First of all, the future witch has to be introduced to the Devil. He is the one who is in charge of the initiation.

This introduction is made by another witch. There were two reasons for the introduction. In the first place, the initiation was supposed to be something like a new baptism for the witch-to-be. And the introducing witch was acting like the godparents at a Christian baptism.

The second reason was one of safety. The introducing witch was vouching for the good intentions of the initiate. And that was a good idea, considering the witch hunts that were going on. After all, the initiate might be an informer. So it was necessary for a regular witch to have checked out the newcomer thoroughly.

Then comes the spoken denial of the Christian Faith. Some common statements were, "I deny my baptism," "I forsake God and Christ," and "I believe in the Devil and adhere to him."

So now the initiate has given up his or her original baptism. Next comes the rebaptism in the Devil's name. Often a new name is given, since he or she has given up a "Christian" name.

Then the Devil is to remove the Christian baptismal markings by touching the subject on the forehead. Then the former godparents are denied, and new sponsors are appointed. The new sponsors must be witches, of course.

Next come the gift of clothing, the oath of allegiance, the writing of the witch's name in the "Book of Death," and the promises to serve the Devil. Along the way, the new witch is marked with the "Devil's Mark."

The Devil's Mark was often later used by the witch hunters to prove that a person was a witch. It was a spot on the body that was rather insensitive to pain. Most of the time, however, the Devil's Mark was really a natural birthmark, a scar, a freckle, a wart, a mole, or even a dimple on the chin.

This is supposed to be the pact that Urbain Grandier, a priest of Loudun, France, made with the Devil. He was accused of witch-craft in 1663. The pact was written back-wards in Latin, and was signed by the Devil and his principal demons.

Sometimes the witch had to sign a paper promising to do the work of the Devil. The signature was often made in blood. There were times when this agreement forced the witch to serve the Devil for the rest of his or her life. But other agreements were good for only a few years. Seven years was the usual number.

So far, we have been talking about changing a person into a witch when the person was willing. But, according to old beliefs, there were ways of making a witch out of an unwilling subject. One of the most common ways involved a couple of types of supernatural creatures. They were the *incubus* and the *succubus*.

An incubus was a male demon sent by the Devil to change women into witches. A succubus was a female demon who did the same job on men.

An incubus approaching a woman. Fifteenth-century print by Ulrich Molitor.

These two types of creatures were supposed to be able to lead humans into sin. And the idea was that after a man or a woman was corrupted by an incubus or a succubus, they would be willing to become a witch.

It is said that the Devil could also make a person a witch by two other methods. Even if the victim refused promises of wealth or power, there were always the tricks of possession or obsession.

In possession, it was said that the Devil sent a demon to get control of a person by force. The demon would take over the mind and body of the victim. This was done by actually entering the body of the person. Anyone who has seen the movie *The Exorcist* is familiar with what happened next. Fortunately, the demon did not usually take over the soul of the person.

There were a lot of crazy things that happened when people were possessed. It was said that their faces and bodies went into fierce contortions. Their expressions were horrible, and their voices turned coarse and gruff. When they talked, their language was either foul or their words could not be understood. They foamed at the mouth. They spit out needles and pins, broken glass, pottery, hair, bark from

Demons trying to tempt a man on his deathbed.

trees, and stones. Worst of all, they were very strong.

Many people had a strange attitude toward a possessed person. Often, they were sympathetic about the whole thing. After all, the possessed person was not to blame. It was the fault of that demon inside.

St. Eligius is taking care of a demon who came to obsess him. Eligius was a bishop in the seventh century and is the patron saint of all metalworkers. That is probably why he is attacking the demon with the tools of his trade.

But they sometimes thought that a really good person could not be possessed by a demon. So there was another explanation. The victim might be obsessed. That means that the demon could not get into the person's body, and might be doing its dirty work on the outside.

One of the most famous cases of obsession was St. Anthony. He was supposed to be tormented by demons. Sometimes these demons took the form of beautiful women. Sometimes they looked like horrible animals. It is said that St. Anthony just spat in their faces.

So there we have it. People could be turned into witches of their own free will. Or if the Devil really wanted a new member of his tribe, he could get one in several ways. He could use an incubus or a succubus. He could use demonic possession. He could use demonic obsession. And if none of those worked, a spell could be put on the victim that would let the demon enter the body and take over, as in possession.

3

FUN AND GAMES

When the witch hunts of the Middle Ages began, people seemed to become more interested in the ceremonies and feasts of witches. Much was made of these gatherings. And the meetings most talked about were the Witches' Sabbaths. This ceremony is often called the sabbat.

The sabbat could be held on any day of the week. But for local meetings, witches seemed to prefer Thursdays and Fridays. The local, small sabbats were something like lodge meetings. That is, they were often held every week.

The most interesting sabbats, however, were the large ones. They were usually held six times a year. There were four seasonal meetings and two meetings to celebrate witches' holidays. They usually began at midnight and didn't finish until dawn.

The first seasonal sabbat of the year was held on February 2. That is, it began at midnight of

A sabbat. In this picture by Breughel the Elder, from the 1500's, we see St. James trying to stop the festivities.

the day of February 1. In the Christian Calendar, this is Candlemas. It should also be pointed out that it is Groundhog Day, too.

The second seasonal sabbat was the spring festival. It was held on June 23. That is the Eve of St. John the Baptist.

The third seasonal sabbat was on August first. This is the summer festival of the Gule of August, which is called Lammas Day in England.

Finally, there was the autumn festival of St. Thomas. It came on December 21.

The two biggest nights of the year, though, were April 30 and October 31. April 30 is the eve of May Day, of course. It is also called Roodmas or Rood Day in England. In Germany it is called *Walpurgisnacht* (Walpurgis Night). The day of St. Walburga, after whom it was named, is the first of May.

But the granddaddy of all witchly celebrations is October 31. That is the date of All Hallows' Eve, or Hallowe'en. Even children still dress up as witches on that night. It is the night when it was believed that the Devil and his witches held their greatest power.

Before the days of Christianity, there was a pagan ritual called *Sanhain*. The Celtic people of the seventh century thought of November first as being the day of death. This was probably so because it marked, for them, the end of autumn. And that meant that it was also the beginning of winter, when even the trees look dead.

So on the evening before—October 31—just before sunset, they started lighting fires. These fires were sacred and were an attempt to stop the sun from going away for the last time in autumn. It never worked, of course. But the ceremony was so popular that the Christians converted it into All Hallows' Eve. It is the night before All Saints' Day.

But now let's get along to the sabbat. It's the big day. Witches came from all over, and that meant that very few of them could walk to the gathering place. A few of them could ride a horse there, but most of them had no means of transportation. So they often had to use witchcraft just to get to the meeting.

What were they supposed to do? Fly, of course. It is said that some of them flew by themselves, although they might have been carried by an invisible demon. Others were said to be supported by a stick or a broom. Still others rode on a flying animal, such as a horse. But it was believed that all of these witchly fliers had to rub a magical ointment on themselves before they could even get off the ground.

Here is a typical recipe for the flying goo:

1. Take the fat from the bodies of young children.
2. Boil the fat in water in a brass pot.
3. Take the thick part of the mixture and add "eleosolinum, aconitum, frondes populeas," and soot.
4. Then add "sium, acarum vulgare, pentaphyllon," the blood of a bat, "solanum somniferum, and oleum."
5. Stamp all these together and smear the ointment on the body.

Off to the sabbat. One witch is flying out of the chimney, three others are preparing to take off, and a curious boy is spying on them.

When riding a stick or a broom or a flying animal, the witch had a choice between two methods. If the stick, broom, or animal were really a demon in disguise, the witch could just hop aboard and fly away. But if the thing in question were really a stick, a broom, or an animal, the witch could use a magic bridle. It would turn the object into a flying machine.

There was a problem, however. Suppose that you were a witch married to a non-witch. It would hardly do just to fly away for the night. How could it be explained to your husband or wife? The only thing to do was to put a spell on anyone who might discover the method of transportation. That is, just put them to sleep for a while. Or, you might put a broom or a stool in your bed. Then you would change the piece of furniture to look like yourself by reciting:

> I lay down this besom in the Devil's name,
> Let it not stir till I come again.

Then off to the sabbat, reciting:

> Horse and hattock,
> Horse and go,
> Horse and pellattis, ho! ho!

You would then go off to the meeting. And on your return, this would be your spell:

> A boy!
> Merry meet,
> Merry part.

And nobody would even know you had left.

Where did the witches meet? The sabbat was usually held in the same place from year to year. Most often it seemed that the meeting place was near a lake, a stream, or a pond. Anyway, it was near some body of water. On the other hand, there were other reports that the meeting was held on top of a mountain or in a clearing in a forest. The point was that the sabbat should be located somewhere away from places where normal people might peek in on the ceremonies.

There were a few popular places. For example, there was a grassy field near Salem, Massachusetts, that was said to be a common meeting place. And there was the Broken Peak in Germany and the top of the Puy-de-Dôme in France. In Sweden, a favorite place was a meadow called the Blocula, or the Blokulla. This place was connected with Sweden's only witch scare, which happened in the seventeenth century.

The whole thing started in the villages of Mora and Älvdalen. A fifteen-year-old boy in Mora, Eric Ericsen, accused several people of stealing children and handing them over to the Devil.

Soon both Mora and Älvdalen were alive with rumors that witches were carrying off young children. The youngsters would be returned the next morning. But they were pale and exhausted. It was said that they had been partaking in "hellish enterprises."

At that time, the king of Sweden was a fourteen-year-old boy, Charles XI. He heard about the happenings, and appointed a committee to investigate.

The committee arrived in Mora in August of 1669. By this time, other children besides Eric had told of their experiences with witches. Seventy adults in the two villages were arrested. Pretty soon, many of the prisoners confessed.

The children gave evidence that sometimes three hundred of them would fly to that meadow. They said it was a field that looked endless. The Devil would baptize them into his service. Then he gave them purses containing parts of clocks. They would have to throw the purses into the water, and swear an oath. "As these filings of the clock do never return to the clock from which they are taken, so may my soul never return to Heaven."

A feast then followed in a nearby house. The witches got to sit near the Devil, but the children had to stand near the door. However, the Devil himself brought their food to them. The menu wasn't too bad—"broth with col-worts and bacon in it, oatmeal, bread spread with butter, milk and cheese."

After that came a dance and a few practical jokes. The Devil let the children ride around him on spits. He sometimes beat them. At other times he would have them build stone walls, which he always knocked over.

All seventy of the accused witches were convicted. Twenty-three of them were behead-ed and their bodies were burned. The other forty-seven were sent to prison. But later they were executed.

Even the children suffered. Fifteen of them were burned to death. Fifty-six others were lashed with rods every Sunday for a year.

There was no special number of witches necessary to hold a sabbat. It is said that an equal number of male and female witches was a good idea, however. But if that was not possible, things could be made equal by getting an incubus or a succubus or two. There were times when non-witches with special connections could be used.

Sabbats were reported with fewer than ten witches present. But there are tales of a sabbat near Ferrara, Italy, with six thousand. That was in the sixteenth century. In the seventeenth century, near Valpute, France, ten thousand showed up.

Here's what might go on at one of these meetings. All the witches have gathered. Some of them have shiny skin because of the ointment they have used. Some of them are holding black candles.

The Devil, or one of his deputy demons, is in charge. He may appear to be a bearded man, a black goat, or even a ram. One description of him told of his having a goat head, human hands, a belly covered with scales, and feathers covering the rest of his body.

He may be seen as a figure with horns, bat wings, and hooves. Or he may be human, but wearing a horned mask and headdress.

The Devil may be sitting on a black throne or standing on an altar. But the witches are gathered around him.

First they renew their vows of obedience. They may present him with gifts, such as black candles. They kiss him, meanwhile bowing and scraping. Then they sing some special hymn that praises the Devil.

In some ways, the sabbat could be compared to a formal business meeting. The next step is like the committee report. Witches tell of all the magic that they have performed since the last sabbat. At the same time, they ask the Devil for hints about how they can carry out their plans for future witchery.

New business comes after that. This includes initiations of new witches. It also may include a wedding between two witches. The Devil performs the ceremony.

Demons can help people, too. It seems here that they could pull wagons, dig in mines, sweep stables, and propel boats. Sixteenth-century woodcut by Olaus Magnus.

The formal part of the sabbat ends with a sacrifice. The common things that were killed were dogs, cats, and chickens.

Then comes the fun part. There is a big banquet. It could be held indoors, or, if the weather was good, it could have taken the form of a picnic.

Sometimes the Devil furnished the food. Sometimes one of the witches brought it. And sometimes each witch would bring his or her basket of goodies. But no matter whose food it was, the witches would say grace to the Devil.

A lot of stories say that the food was really disgusting. And that no matter how much a witch ate, his or her appetite was not satisfied. But other reports tell of sumptuous feasts. There were wines and liquors, huge platters of meat, and other dainties. Of course, it was often said that the meat came from stolen babies.

No salt was used, since salt is supposed to be unlucky for witches. Also, the witches never used knives or forks. Not that they were sloppy—it was just that iron is also used to put hexes on witches, and most people could not afford silver tableware at that time.

Once the banquet was over, the dancing started. Sometimes they danced simple country dances. But more often the dances were magical ones. There were jumping dances that made the crops grow higher. There were fertility dances that increased the birth rate. And the witches could dress up like animals and perform a dance to increase the number of domestic animals to be born.

The magic dances were usually of two types. One was a sort of ring dance. It was danced around a stone, a maypole, or even the Devil himself. The witches often danced back to back in this one, and it was always danced counterclockwise.

The second type of dance might have looked

On with the dance. Festivities at the sabbat.

like a game of follow-the-leader. These were the really wild fast dances. There were stories of a witch or two who were punished because they couldn't keep up with the others. The Devil was supposed to beat on the slow witch at the end of the line. This is possibly where our saying, "The Devil take the hind-most," came from.

The music for the dancing consisted of both singing and instrumental playing. The instruments most often used were Pipes of Pan, Jew's harps, or some other simple mouth instruments. Tambourines were also used. There were times when the Devil would provide the music. The songs that were sung usually had wicked language in them. But they were sung in praise of the Devil.

The singing and dancing went on all night. But at the first crowing of a rooster at dawn, the witches would go home.

Some students of the history of witchcraft tell of other types of meetings called esbats. The esbat was strictly business, unlike the sabbat, which was more of a religious festival.

The esbat's purpose was for a whole group of witches to work out plans for doing harm. Sometimes they were held in order to open graves to steal the bones of dead men, women, and children. These could then be used for magic charms.

Witches could raise storms. Sixteenth-century woodcut by Olaus Magnus.

Esbats were also called for blasphemous purposes. A cat or some other animal would be christened. Other purposes for the meeting might be planning a campaign against a human being, wrecking a ship, or getting a fellow witch out of prison.

A little fun could be plotted at such a meeting. Perhaps they were meeting just to create a thunderstorm that would wash out a picnic or rain on a parade.

Esbats were not large meetings. At least not as large as the sabbats. They were usually held on a certain day of the week, but there was no fixed hour. Some of them were even held in the daylight hours. It was the Devil who was supposed to set the day and the hour. He told his followers about it personally or sent around a message with an officer of the group. And then the magic began.

4
OTHER SPORTS

It has been mentioned before that witches were big on causing crops to fail and animals to stop reproducing. In fact, the man who started the whole big witch hunt, Pope Innocent VII, made a statement about that in 1488.

He described witches as being those "who blight the marriage bed, destroy the births of women, and prevent the increase of cattle; they blast the corn on the ground, the grapes of the vineyard, the fruits of the trees, and the grass and herbs of the field." That's quite a statement.

When Queen Elizabeth I was ruling England, a new cattle disease popped up. The cows were going blind. Witches called "eye-biters" were blamed and then executed.

Anyone can see how causing animals and crops to die is a typical witch's trick. It causes great hardship, after all. But how can increasing the number of cattle and fertility of crops be called the work of the Devil?

For one thing, extra fertility means that there will be more food for the witches to eat. And causing a field to become fertile may cause some damage. Extra fertility means that more weeds and brambles will also grow in the field. They might crowd out the crop. This is a pretty nasty joke on the farmer.

Still and all, witches were convenient people to have around. At least for the superstitious. Some "normal" people went to witches to get love potions. These could be used to trap a future husband or wife. On the other hand, a witch could sell you poison. Or take a look into the future for you.

A male witch selling some sailors a wind that is tied up in a rope. Sixteenth-century woodcut by Olaus Magnus.

You could also get a witch to give someone the "evil eye." All that the witch had to do was to look your enemy in the eye. This would bewitch or even kill him or her.

The evil eye could cause disease, it was said. It was able to split mirrors or jewels. It could knock birds out of the sky.

There were tales of children being enchanted by the evil eye. But there was supposed to be a way of telling whether or not this had happened.

Take three small apples and drop them into a pan of water. Now put the pan and the apples under the child's bed. If the apples float, the child is not a victim of the evil eye. If they sink, too bad.

Another method involves the use of a piece of bread. Cut it with a knife that has been marked with three crosses. Then leave the bread and the knife on the child's pillow all night. Look at the knife in the morning. If there is rust on it, the child is enchanted.

The easiest method is to lick the forehead of the child. If it tastes salty, the youngster is a victim of the evil eye.

Another power that witches were supposed to have was that of changing themselves into animals. These animals could be of any shape or size. But most often the witch would choose a dog, a cat, a rabbit, a toad, or a bird. The point was to turn into something common, not something horrible. That way, the witch was less likely to be noticed.

If nobody noticed the animal, it was helpful to the witch. It made it much easier for him or her to do some dirty work. And it also made it much easier to get into somebody's home—to fly in through the window as a bird, or crawl under the door as an insect.

Some people thought that this power was not given to all witches. There were only a few who so pleased the Devil that he would grant them this ability. Of course, it was believed that at special times the Devil could turn any witch into any kind of animal.

One little verse that was supposed to help a witch turn into a rabbit was:

> *I shall go into a hare,*
> *With sorrow and such and mickle care;*
> *And I shall go in the Devil's name*
> *Until I come home again.*

Witches were also closely identified with animals in another way. These animals were the witches' *familiars*. There were two kinds. One was the *divining familiar*, and was used by the witch to foretell the future. The other was the *domestic familiar,* and this was really a servant of the witch.

The divining familiar was not the property of the witch. Some people thought that this type of familiar was really the Devil in disguise. At any rate, it usually showed up only at magical ceremonies.

When it did show up, it was said that the witch could read the future by looking at it. It was necessary to notice from what direction it had come. Its speed and actions were also important. There were reports of the familiar turning into its Devil's shape and telling the witch about the future.

Domestic familiars were also called familiar spirits and familiar imps. They were the personal property of the witch. And each witch usually had only one. They were used to help

A witch and some of the animals that could become her familiar.

the witch make magic. And they sometimes acted as servants. This kind of familiar was sort of a household helper.

The familiar was usually supposed to be a small animal. And the witch could keep it in a pot or a box. At the bottom of the container was a bed made of wool.

The quickest way for a witch to get a familiar was to have the Devil give it as a present. Often it was given at the initiation. If the gift was a divining familiar, of course, the Devil would take it back. In this case, he was just showing the witch what kind of familiar to look for so that the witch could keep it as his or her very own.

If the gift was a domestic familiar, the witch could keep it. And special directions for its care and feeding were given. Also, the special powers of that particular familiar would be explained.

One witch could give a familiar to another witch. These were domestic familiars, of course. And they were sometimes passed on from one generation to the next. A mother witch could give one to her daughter witch. A father witch could give one to his son witch.

Much has been written about the power of witches' spells. Spells are just words that are supposed to have magical powers. But there are several types of them that were supposed to have been used by witches.

The first kind of spell called on the protection of the Devil or one of his demons. Actually, non-witches have always used this kind of spell to call for the aid of God or some of his saints. One of the most common examples is:

> *Matthew, Mark, Luke, and John,*
> *Bless the bed that I lie on.*

There were spells that were used for some minor magic act, like making a love potion. But, the most powerful spell of all was used to raise the Devil in person.

One witch confessed that she raised the Devil by saying, "Benedicite." When she wanted him to go away, she said, "Maikpeblis."

A witch crossing the sea by means of a spell. Sixteenth-century woodcut by Olaus Magnus.

Another witch raised the Devil with "Serpent." Still another cried, "Robin."

To summon her familiar, one witch claimed to have shouted, "Elva." Her particular familiar was a dog. When she wanted him to go away, she said, "Depart by the law you live on." This was the same witch who confessed that she caused storms by throwing a cat into the ocean, shouting, "Hail, hola."

Finally, here is an example of a witch's grace before dinner. Remember that she was a Devil worshipper. So she is praying to Satan.

We eat this meat in the Devil's name
With sorrow, and such, and meikle shame;
We shall destroy house and hall,
Both sheep and goat until the fall.
Little good shall come to the fore.
Of all the rest of the little store.

But after the meal, if she wanted to get rid of the Devil, she could. Here is a popular little statement to send him on his way. "I am pleased and contented with thee, Prince Lucifer, for the moment. Leave thou in peace now, and go in quiet and without trouble. Do not forget our pact, or I shall blast thee with my wand."

King James VI of Scotland having some witches beaten.

5

WITCH CONTROL

Those people who believed in witches needed ways to fight them, of course. And, before the days of the full-scale witch hunt, there were simple methods that were used.

To begin with, the people thought that you could break a witch's spell by beating her. One of the most popular weapons for this was a whip made of elder wood or mountain ash. And witches were not supposed to be able to get near garlic, bay branches, or witch hazel. They were also supposed to be afraid of holy water.

Stones could come in handy, too. Take a stone with a hole in it. String it around your neck, and you are safe. That same stone could be nailed to your door and it would protect the whole house.

There were other ways to protect a house from witches. Hang horseshoes or the metal parts of a horse's bridle over the door. Hang green glass balls in the windows. Bury an iron knife under the doorstep. Remember, witches cannot stand iron.

One rather violent stunt used to harm a witch could be done only on Hallowe'en. It used to be popular to burn cats on that night. A cat was supposed to be either a witch's familiar or the witch herself.

Suppose you had had a spell put on you by a witch. Also, suppose that the witch lived in a house with a tile roof. You could just steal a piece of tile, pour salt on it, and heat it. That would cancel out the spell.

The Church had ways of dealing with witch-

es and people who were thought to be possessed by a demon. They could be exorcised.
That is, the demon could be persuaded to get
out of the body of the victim. Remember the
film, *The Exorcist?*

The ceremony sometimes took the form of a
talk between a priest and the demon. The
demon would lie and curse and try to make the
priest give up. The priest would recite prayers

*A priest of the Middle Ages exorcising a demon out of a
possessed person.*

and argue with the demon. He would also sprinkle the possessed person with holy water and hold a crucifix on him or her.

If exorcism did not work, there was another method called fumigation. The priest first drew a picture of the demon. Then he made the sign of the cross over the picture and put holy water on it. Then the picture was thrown into the fire. Sometimes these ceremonies would go on for months.

Exorcism is not too common today. A Roman Catholic priest must get the permission of his bishop to do it. Eastern Orthodox priests may do it from time to time. The last mention of the rite in Anglican Church history goes back to the time of Edward the VI, in the mid-sixteenth century. Most Protestant groups either never had it or gave it up long ago.

There were nonreligious forms of exorcism in the old days, too. Sometimes people would throw stones at the person who was thought to be possessed. Sometimes he or she was beaten with leather straps. These methods were used

An old engraving showing how men regarded women. These five women obviously have been affected by the moon.

to frighten the demon out of the body.

Another way had to do with food. A curse was put on a piece of meat and fed to the victim. Then the possessed person was made to vomit out the meat. Supposedly, the demon would come out with the food.

As mentioned before, people really began to get upset about witches at the beginning of the Middle Ages. That is when the witchcraft trials really began.

6

THE WITCH HUNT

The beginning of the witch hunt can probably be traced to the early thirteenth century, although the worst part of it occurred almost two centuries later. It was then that the Holy Inquisition was created by the Roman Catholic Church. The leaders of the Church believed that they were surrounded by heretics. And anyone who did not believe in the Church's teachings must be a worshipper of the Devil and a witch.

The first persecutions were begun at that time against a group called the Manichaeans.

They were also called the Albigensians, since they were headquartered in Albi, France. This group believed in a god that was both good and evil. This was clearly a denial of church teaching. The group was almost exterminated.

At about the same time, another group was attacked. It was also a French group, and was called the Waldensians, or the Vadois, because their leader was named Waldo. Waldo was a merchant in the town of Lyons, and was famous for giving away most of his goods to the poor.

His followers believed in the Bible. But they

One artist's idea of what the Devil looked like standing in front of the mouth of Hell. Fifteenth-century woodcut by Jacobus de Teramo.

It was a time of fear. Evil forces were every-where. Even with his family and priests nearby, a man in his own bed in his own home could be tempted by demons. Fifteenth-century woodcut.

did not believe that the Pope had any authority. The Inquisition killed many of them, but there were those who were able to escape to the Piedmont Region in the foothills of the Alps Mountains.

They were later persecuted by the Inquisition in the fifteenth century. This time they were not only accused of being Waldensians, but also of being witches. Still, some of them managed to survive. Today, some of their descendants can still be found in the Piedmont.

So, early on, people who were called heretics were thought of as being witches. Heretics are those who do not believe in the teachings of the established church.

Perhaps the first person to be executed for witchcraft by the Inquisition was a woman accused of living with the Devil. She was sentenced to be burned in Toulouse, France, in 1275.

Another witch trial occurred in 1436. Thomas Bègue was the accused. He confessed that he had conjured up a demon named Mermet by calling out, "Mermet *diable!*" three times. The demon then appeared as a black cat and immediately changed his shape into an old man dressed in black with horns on his feet.

In the fifteenth century, the French Inquisition, with a little help from the cruel King Philip IV, attacked the Order of the Knights Templar. The Templars were founded about 1118, during the Crusades, as a kind of holy army. But they were accused of being witches, and fifty-four of them were burned at the stake. The Inquisition by the way, took over the wealth of the order.

But the real beginning of the terror occurred in 1486. A book was published called *Malleus Maleficarum,* or *The Hammer of Witches.* It was written by two German Inquisitors, Jacob Sprenger and Heinrich Kramer, and was a handbook for witch hunters.

It described witchcraft, told of what witches were supposed to do, and explained Devil

This is a heretic who has been condemned to death. His tunic is decorated with the faces of demons. Eighteenth-century engraving.

worship. Other things that it mentioned were the nature of demons, why women were more often witches than men were, and the ways in which humans were affected by witches.

The book went on to tell how to convict witches in the courts. And here is a bit about how that was done.

The first point to remember is that the

accused person was to be considered guilty until she could prove herself to be innocent. Think for a minute about that. She would have to prove that something had *not* happened. And that is next to impossible. No matter how much she claimed she had not done anything, there were enough superstitious and hysterical people around who would swear that she was lying.

Next, it was usual for the accused not to have a defense attorney. In the first place, it was thought if you defended a witch, you must be a witch yourself. In the second place, even if the witch could find a courageous lawyer, she still would probably lose the case. So both she and the attorney were liable to be executed.

Torture was often used to get a confession. But torture was not always necessary.

Gossip was often enough to get a woman arrested. Anyone who was seen to throw water out of a bucket might be accused of trying to cause a storm with witchcraft. All a woman had to be was old, ugly, or deformed, and she might be accused of being a witch. But that didn't let the pretty young women off the hook. They might be called "bewitching" young ladies, and thus be arrested.

If a woman had a pet in the house, she might be accused of witchcraft. There were people who would swear that the pet was her familiar. Even if the woman did not have a pet, she might be tied up in an empty room. Then the judges would watch her through a peephole to see if a familiar animal would visit her.

Think of the filth that must have existed in a medieval jail, or even a medieval home. It is not hard to see that if the judges waited long enough, a rat or a spider or an insect would eventually pay a call on the prisoner. That was proof that she was a witch.

Another method of testing for witchiness was to duck the prisoner. In most cases of ducking, the right thumb was tied to the left big toe. Then the accused was thrown into the water. If

The "swimming test" of the 1500's. The accused witch has been tied in a cloth bag before being thrown into the water.

she sank, she was not a witch. If she floated, she was. The reason for that idea was that the water was trying to reject the witch. After all, she had rejected the holy water used in her original baptism. It should be pointed out that the person who sank—the one who was supposed to be innocent—often drowned.

A popular way of testing the prisoner was through the use of *bibliomancy*. The accused was put on one end of a weighing scale, and the

Bible from the local church was put on the other end. If the woman weighed less than the Bible, she was innocent. But how many times could that have happened?

The judges would also look for witch's marks or the Devil's Mark on the body of the prisoner. Any kind of spot could be called a mark by these judges. Very few people lack at least one mole, birthmark, wart, or scar on their bodies. So the judges were usually able to find a mark, and the accused was convicted.

There was also the test called "pricking." When the mark was found, it was pricked with a pin. If it didn't hurt or bleed, it was a true witch's mark or Devil's Mark.

A few people passed the test, so the judges thought up the idea of the invisible mark. They were then free to stick pins anywhere on the body of the prisoner. Even though there was no mark to be seen, if the place did not hurt or bleed, there was a ghostly mark there some-place. It wasn't hard to find these invisible marks. Many parts of our bodies are almost pain- and blood-free. Two examples are the skin on our heels or some old scar.

It was also possible that, by the time the pin was used, the accused would not feel pain. After having been stripped in public, perhaps shaved, probably tortured, who would notice a little pin prick?

Just to be sure, some judges were said to use fake needles. These were fixed so that when the point touched anything, the needle would slide back up into a handle.

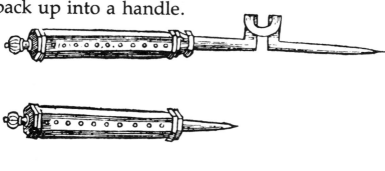

Prickers were used to find the "Devil's Mark." The two at the bottom have the famous retractable blade, which caused neither pain nor bleeding.

Matthew Hopkins with two witches and their familiars. Notice the names of the animals. Seventeenth-century woodcut.

It seemed as though there were always people around who would accuse someone of being a witch. Some of them, no doubt, really believed in witchcraft. Others were just spiteful. Still others were paid by the court.

One of these people paid by the court was the infamous Matthew Hopkins—the Witch Finder. He was an Englishman who lived in the seventeenth century.

Hopkins' first big success was the sending to trial of thirty-two accused witches in Chelmsford, Sussex. Then he started to tour through Eastern England, accusing people of being witches wherever he went.

His favorite ways of making the victims confess were ducking, pricking, starvation, and prevention of sleep. Finally, the authorities began to doubt his methods and he was forced to retire. But he had been responsible for more executions in his fourteen months of activity than all the other English prosecutors in the previous one hundred sixty years.

By the way, the typical sentence for a convicted witch in Europe was burning. In England and the American Colonies, it was hanging.

Consider the famous Salem witch hunt in Massachusetts. The nine-year-old daughter of the minister of the church there, Elizabeth Parris, and some of her friends began behaving strangely. They would laugh, then cry, and then seem to be having fits. Some of them

The Salem girls listening to ghost stories told by Tituba, the servant of the Reverend Parris. They later accused her of being a witch. Nineteenth-century drawing.

A Salem girl is "possessed" in court. From Harper's Magazine, *1892.*

crawled around on the floor and tried to bite people in the ankle.

They said that they were bewitched, and accused three people of the town of being witches. One of the people was hanged. Another died in jail. The third was kept in jail for over a year and then sold as a slave. Before it was over in Salem, one hundred forty-one people were accused, thirty-one were convicted, and twenty were hanged.

The history of the trials is a history of cruelty, ignorance, and superstition. As everyone knows, no matter how saintly a person was, he or she could still be condemned for witchcraft. The story of Joan of Arc is but the most prominent example in a long line of tragic trials.

7

SOME REAL
EXPLANATIONS

The witch hunts occurred during a time of great superstition. There were people who wanted to be witches, but many more were unjustly accused. It was easy for people to believe that anyone who was a little different could either be a witch or be possessed or obsessed by a demon.

The person who laughed too much might be bewitched. The person who appreciated beauty too much might be bewitched. The person who walked in his or her sleep might be bewitched. The person who was dull-witted or ugly might be bewitched. In short, anyone who was not quite the same as everyone else might be bewitched.

Remember the description of the actions of a possessed person. The face and body are contorted. The person has a fiendish expression and twitches all the time. The voice is coarse and gruff. The language is foul or may be only gibberish. The person may foam at the mouth. And he or she may vomit needles and pins, broken glass or pottery, hair, bark, and stone.

Let's face it. Anyone who acts that way may be putting on an act. It might be a way of excusing away a person's misdeeds if he or she were caught. It might be a way of saying, "It really wasn't my fault. I was possessed by a demon." Or, to put it another way: "The Devil made me do it."

But the chances are that there was really something wrong with the people who behaved like that. They really weren't witches, of course, even if they thought they were. However, they were suffering from something. Let's take a look at some of the explanations.

To begin with, they may have been suffering from the psychological problem called *hysteria*. Those symptoms are common to hysterics. And that includes the vomiting of strange objects. Hysterics often have the desire to swallow things and then vomit them up.

Now let's take obsession and possession. Obsession is a state of mind in which the patient has a fixed idea that is not normal. He or she thinks that there is a demon trying to do harm. He or she might fear that something is trying to get power over his or her mind and body. This sounds a lot like a mental illness called *paranoia*.

In the case of possession, a demon is supposed to be occupying the body of the victim. There is an explanation for this, too. The people who were possessed may have been suffering from a mental illness called *schizophrenia (skit-so-FREE-nya)*.

Victims of this disease lose contact with reality. They may lose their own personality so much that they believe themselves to be, at times, another person.

Another possible disease that a "witch" might have had is epilepsy. Some types of this disease are so mild that the symptoms may be only a brief loss of awareness. Others, such as the type called *grand mal*, involve violent fits. The victim may lose consciousness, thrash about wildly, foam at the mouth, and bite the tongue. After the seizure, the person may be confused and remember nothing about the attack. That sounds quite a bit like the symptoms of being bewitched.

Another rather rare disease is Tourette's Syndrome. The disease generally begins in childhood, usually between two and fourteen years of age. The first symptoms are tics, or involuntary muscle movements, in the face and other parts of the body. The victims may also kick and stamp their feet.

Sometimes the person makes awful faces without knowing why. Often the victim makes noises without having any control over his or her speech. These noises may be grunts, shouts, barks, throat clearing, or sighing. The sufferer may also curse and swear involuntarily. Doesn't that sound like someone who might be "possessed"?

Then there is the disease known as Huntington's Chorea. It is a particularly tragic disease. The symptoms come on slowly, and most victims do not know they have the disease until they are past thirty years of age. By that time, they probably have had children. Since Huntington's Chorea is an inherited disease, they may already have passed it on to their sons and daughters.

The symptoms include involuntary body movements and peculiar or strange behavior. Intelligence is affected. The sufferer often gets irritable and has fits of anger and temper. He or she may laugh loudly for no reason at all. The victim may babble like a baby, scream, grunt, or just talk for hours on end.

Eventually, the victims go so far downhill mentally and physically that they die. But the symptoms make them appear to a believer in witchcraft as though they had been possessed by a demon.

So much for diseases. Is there a possibility that drugs had anything to do with some of the witch occurrences of the past?

Recently, some scientists have come up with the idea that the witches of Salem in 1692 may have been only hallucinations. The young girls who accused people of being witches may have just eaten some contaminated bread. They may have had what is called *convulsive ergotism.*

The culprit was a fungus called *ergot* that had infected the rye used in making bread. The symptoms of ergotism are crawling sensations in the skin, tingling in the fingers, dizziness, headaches, and hallucinations. This can be explained by pointing out that ergot contains a

hallucinogen related to LSD. Perhaps that ex-
plains the weird behavior of the girls.

Let's look at the way some witches were
supposed to use chemicals. The most prominent mixtures were those that were used for
flying ointments. Basically, there were three
recipes:

1. Parsley, water of aconite, poplar leaves, and soot.
2. Water parsnip, sweet flag, cinquefoil, bat's blood,
   deadly nightshade, and oil.
3. Baby's fat, juice of water parsnip, aconite, cinquefoil,
   deadly nightshade, and soot.

Now, aconite and deadly nightshade (belladonna) are two of the three most poisonous
plants that can be found in Europe. The third
one is hemlock. And there is a possibility that
the parsley in the formula was really hemlock.

Aconite slows down the heartbeat and may
cause excessive excitement. Belladonna and
hemlock cause excitement and delirious
dreams.

So recipe number one would cause you to be

mentally confused, with slowed-down movements, irregular heartbeats, dizziness, and shortness of breath. Recipe number two would make you excited and delirious. Recipe number three would make you excited and give you irregular heartbeats.

You can forget that other stuff about bat's blood and baby fat. But you must remember that the witches did not eat the ointment. That would have killed them. They rubbed it on their bodies, and perhaps some of it got through the skin into the bloodstream.

So that's the science of witches. At least now we can explain some of the strange goings-on. And because of our knowledge we can be sure that there will never be another period like that of the witch hunt, with its hysterical persecutions and tortures and executions.

Or can we . . . ?

OTHER BOOKS
ABOUT WITCHES

Aylesworth, Thomas G. *Servants of the Devil*. Reading, Massachusetts: Addison-Wesley Publishing Company, Incorporated, 1970.

Carus, Paul. *The Devil and the Idea of Evil*. New York: Bell Publishing Company, 1969.

de Givry, Grillot. *Witchcraft, Magic & Alchemy*. New York: Dover Publications, Incorporated, 1971.

Epstein, Perle. *The Way of Witches*. Garden City, New York: Doubleday & Company, Incorporated, 1972.

Hill, Douglas, and Pat Williams. *The Supernatural*. New York: Hawthorn Books, Incorporated, 1965.

————, et al. *Witchcraft, Magic and the Supernatural*. London: Octopus Books Limited, 1974.

Kingston, Jeremy. *Witches and Witchcraft*. Garden City, New York: Doubleday & Company, Incorporated, 1976.

Landsburg, Alan. *In Search of . . .* Garden City, New York: Nelson Doubleday, Incorporated, 1978.

Lethbridge, T.C. *Witches*. New York: The Citadel Press, 1962.

Maple, Eric. *The Dark World of Witches*. New York: Castle Books, 1964.

―――. *The Domain of Devils*. New York: A. S. Barnes and Company, Incorporated, 1966.

Michelet, Jules. *Satanism and Witchcraft*. New York: The Citadel Press, 1939.

Nauman, St. Elmo, Jr. (ed.). *Exorcism Through the Ages*. New York: Philosophical Library, 1974.

Robotti, Frances Diane. *Chronicles of Old Salem*. New York: Bonanza Books, 1948.

Starkey, Marion L. *The Devil in Massachusetts*. Garden City, New York: Anchor Books, 1969.

Summers, Montague. *The History of Witchcraft*. New Hyde Park, New York: University Books, 1956.

Trachtenberg, Joshua. *Jewish Magic and Superstition*. New York: Behrman's Jewish Book House, 1939.

Upham, Charles W. *Salem Witchcraft* (Volumes One and Two). New York: Frederick Ungar Publishing Company, 1867.

Watson, Lyall. *Supernature*. Garden City, New York: Doubleday & Company, Incorporated, 1973.

Wedeck, Harry E. *A Treasury of Witchcraft*. New York: Philosophical Library, 1961.

INDEX